WELCOME TO THE U.S.A.
ILLINOIS

Written by Ann Heinrichs Illustrated by Matt Kania
Content Adviser: Karen Egan, Youth Services Consultant,
Illinois State Library, Springfield, Illinois

The Child's World

Published in the United States of America by The Child's World®
PO Box 326 • Chanhassen, MN 55317-0326
800-599-READ • www.childsworld.com

Photo Credits

Cover: Brand X Pictures; frontispiece: Getty Images/The Image Bank/
Tim Bieber.

Interior: Vicki Byers/Deere & Company, Moline, Illinois: 33; Cahokia Mounds
State Historic Site: 9; Corbis: 14 (Richard Hamilton Smith), 17 (Richard Cummins);
Getty Images: 19 (Photodisc/John A. Rizzo), 22 (Andy Hayt/NBAE), 24 (Tim
Boyle), 34 (Hulton|Archive); Deborah Guzman/Fermilab: 26; Illinois Department
of Natural Resources: 11; Lakeview Museum of Arts and Sciences: 28; David
Lewis/Great American Popcorn Company: 30; Library of Congress: 12; Lincoln's
New Salem: 13; Shawnee National Forest: 6; Jim Woodring/The Squirrel Lover's
Club: 20.

Acknowledgments

The Child's World®: Mary Berendes, Publishing Director

Editorial Directions, Inc.: E. Russell Primm, Editorial Director; Katie Marsico, Associate
Editor; Judith Shiffer, Assistant Editor; Matt Messbarger, Editorial Assistant; Susan
Hindman, Copy Editor; Melissa McDaniel, Proofreader; Peter Garnham, Matt
Messbarger, Olivia Nellums, Chris Simms, Molly Symmonds, Katherine Trickle, Carl
Stephen Wender, Fact Checkers; Tim Griffin/IndexServ, Indexer; Cian Loughlin O'Day,
Photo Researcher and Editor

The Design Lab: Kathleen Petelinsek, Design and art production

Library of Congress Cataloging-in-Publication Data
Heinrichs, Ann.
  Illinois / written by Ann Heinrichs ; cartography and illustrations by Matt Kania.
    p. cm. — (Welcome to the U.S.A.)
  Includes index.
  ISBN 1-59296-285-8 (library bound : alk. paper)
  1. Illinois—Juvenile literature. 2. Illinois—Geography—Juvenile literature. I. Kania, Matt.
II. Title. III. Series.
  F541.3.H45 2004
  977.3—dc22   2004005709

Ann Heinrichs is the author of more than 100 books for children and young adults. She has also enjoyed successful careers as a children's book editor and an advertising copywriter. Ann grew up in Fort Smith, Arkansas, and lives in Chicago, Illinois.

About the Author
Ann Heinrichs

Matt Kania loves maps and, as a kid, dreamed of making them. In school he studied geography and cartography, and today he makes maps for a living. Matt's favorite thing about drawing maps is learning about the places they represent. Many of the maps he has created can be found in books, magazines, videos, Web sites, and public places.

About the Map Illustrator
Matt Kania

On the cover: Chicago's skyscrapers light up as the sun goes down.
On page one: Fishers enjoy Illinois's rivers and lakes.

OUR ILLINOIS TRIP

Illinois's Nicknames: The Land of Lincoln and the Prairie State

Are you ready to explore Illinois? Just follow that dotted line. Or jump in anywhere along the way. Whatever's your idea of fun, you'll find it here. You'll ride a train and paddle a canoe. You'll see dinosaurs and count squirrels. You'll meet Abraham Lincoln and the world's tallest man. So buckle up! Illinois, here we come!

WELCOME TO
ILLINOIS

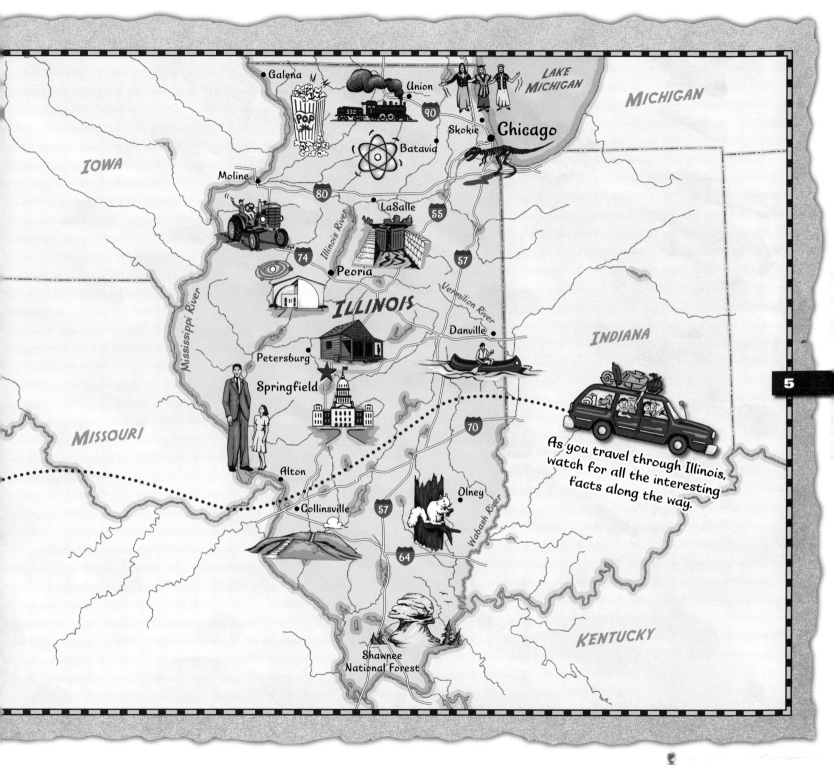

IOWA

Galena

Union

POP

332

Moline

80

LaSalle

74

Peoria

ILLINOIS

Petersburg

Springfield

Alton

Collinsville

57

Shawnee
National Forest

Batavia

Skokie

Chicago

LAKE
MICHIGAN

MICHIGAN

55

57

Danville

INDIANA

70

64

Olney

Mississippi River

Illinois River

Vermilion River

Wabash River

MISSOURI

KENTUCKY

90

As you travel through Illinois,
watch for all the interesting
facts along the way.

6

The Garden of the Gods

See any interesting shapes? The Garden of the Gods contains incredible rock formations.

Illinois's plains were once grasslands called prairies. That's why Illinois is called the Prairie State.

Here's a monkey face. There's a camel's back. This is no zoo. It's the Garden of the Gods. It's in the Shawnee Hills of southern Illinois. All those critters are huge rocks!

Hills, valleys, and rocky cliffs cover southern Illinois. But most of the state is rolling plains. These plains make rich farmland.

Northeastern Illinois faces Lake Michigan. That's one of the nation's five Great Lakes. Sandy beaches and sand dunes line the lake.

The Mississippi River forms Illinois's western border. The Ohio River runs along southeastern Illinois. It joins the Mississippi River near Cairo.

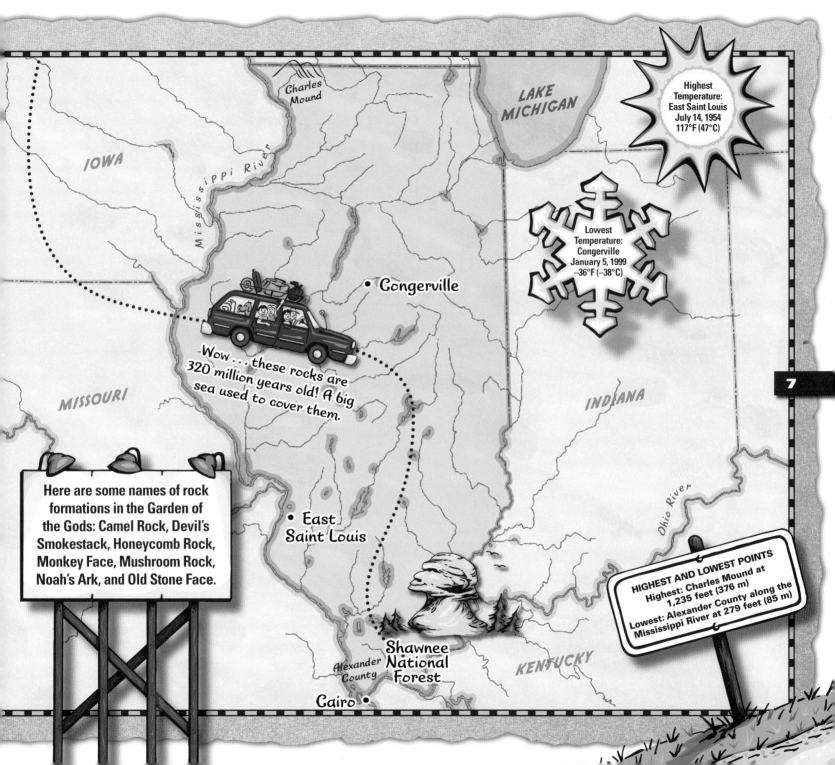

Highest Temperature:
East Saint Louis
July 14, 1954
117°F (47°C)

Lowest Temperature:
Congerville
January 5, 1999
−36°F (−38°C)

Charles Mound

IOWA

LAKE MICHIGAN

Mississippi River

Congerville

INDIANA

MISSOURI

Wow . . . these rocks are 320 million years old! A big sea used to cover them.

Ohio River

East Saint Louis

Here are some names of rock formations in the Garden of the Gods: Camel Rock, Devil's Smokestack, Honeycomb Rock, Monkey Face, Mushroom Rock, Noah's Ark, and Old Stone Face.

Shawnee National Forest

Alexander County

KENTUCKY

HIGHEST AND LOWEST POINTS
Highest: Charles Mound at
1,235 feet (376 m)
Lowest: Alexander County along the
Mississippi River at 279 feet (85 m)

Cairo

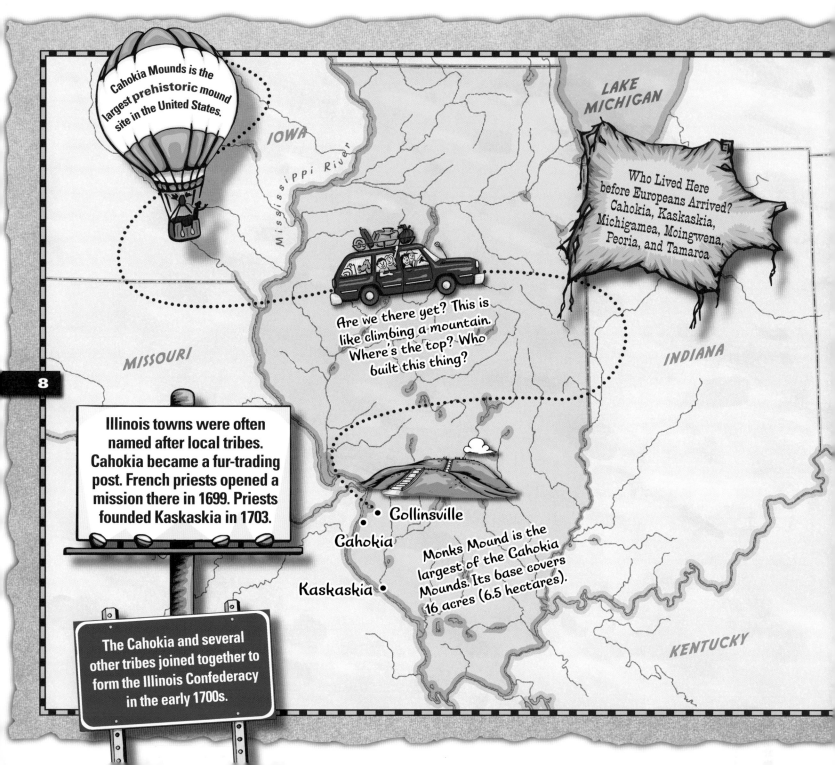

Monks Mound and the Cahokia People

A model of a Cahokia village awaits you. See it at the Cahokia Mounds Visitor Center.

Monks Mound is a huge hill near Collinsville. Cahokia people built it out of earth. It's as high as a ten-story building! You can't drive to the top, though. You have to walk.

The Cahokia lived 1,000 years ago. Their big city had many streets and homes. The mounds were for important buildings and ceremonies. A few were used for **burials.**

Many Native American groups once lived in Illinois. Jacques Marquette and Louis Jolliet arrived in 1673. They were French explorers from Canada. They came down the Mississippi River in canoes. Later, French settlers moved into the area. Fur traders came, too. They traded with the American Indians for animal skins.

Collinsville has the world's largest ketchup bottle. It's really a water tower. It could hold several hundred thousand bottles of ketchup.

Thousands of men worked on the canal. It took them 12 years to build.

Canal boats were flat boats called barges. Barges were tied to mules that walked along the shore.

S queak! The gates swing open. Whoosh! The water gushes in. Squawk! The gates crank shut. What a way to travel!

You're watching Lock 14 at LaSalle. It was part of the Illinois and Michigan Canal. People dug the canal to make a waterway. It connected Lake Michigan to the Mississippi River. Locks held the water back. Their gates opened and shut. This moved the water to a higher or lower level.

Illinois became a state in 1818. Then thousands of settlers moved in. Some raised corn, pigs, and cattle. Others worked in factories or mines. They shipped their goods on canals. That was much faster than traveling by land.

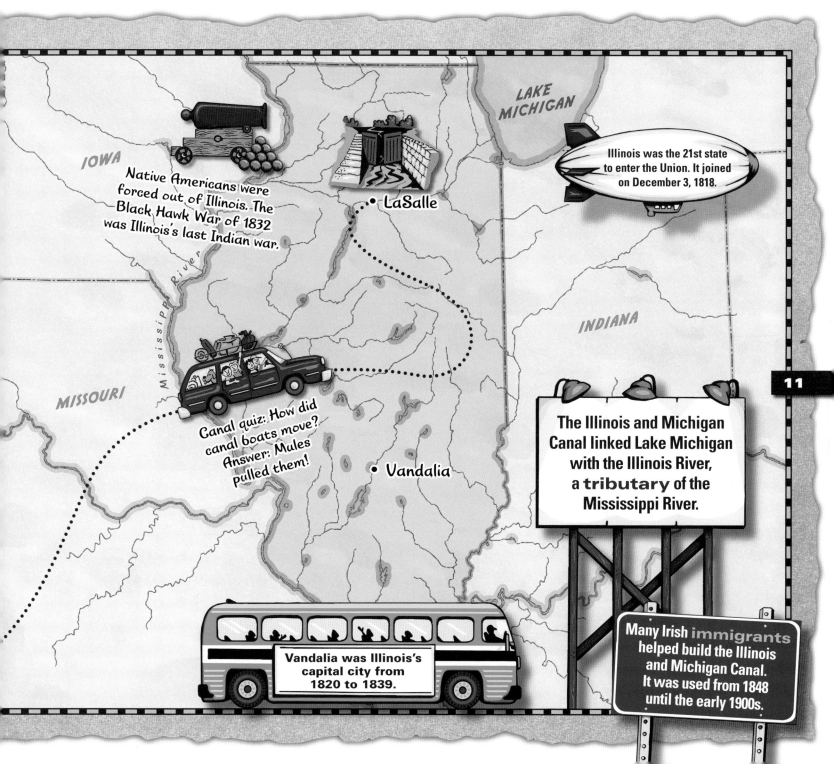

IOWA

Native Americans were forced out of Illinois. The Black Hawk War of 1832 was Illinois's last Indian war.

LAKE MICHIGAN

Illinois was the 21st state to enter the Union. It joined on December 3, 1818.

• LaSalle

MISSOURI

Mississippi River

Canal quiz: How did canal boats move? Answer: Mules pulled them!

INDIANA

• Vandalia

The Illinois and Michigan Canal linked Lake Michigan with the Illinois River, a **tributary** of the Mississippi River.

Vandalia was Illinois's capital city from 1820 to 1839.

Many Irish **immigrants** helped build the Illinois and Michigan Canal. It was used from 1848 until the early 1900s.

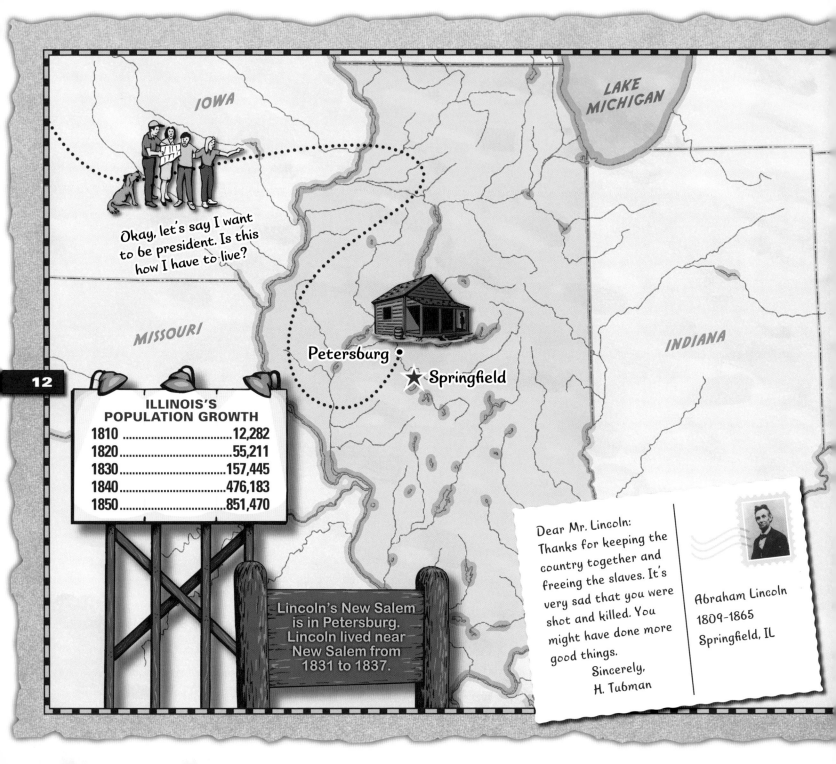

Okay, let's say I want to be president. Is this how I have to live?

ILLINOIS'S POPULATION GROWTH

1810	12,282
1820	55,211
1830	157,445
1840	476,183
1850	851,470

IOWA

LAKE MICHIGAN

MISSOURI

INDIANA

Petersburg

★ Springfield

Lincoln's New Salem is in Petersburg. Lincoln lived near New Salem from 1831 to 1837.

Dear Mr. Lincoln:
Thanks for keeping the country together and freeing the slaves. It's very sad that you were shot and killed. You might have done more good things.
          Sincerely,
          H. Tubman

Abraham Lincoln
1809-1865
Springfield, IL

You're hungry? Grow some vegetables! You're out of soap? Make some! You're at summer camp in Lincoln's New Salem. It's your chance to see how Abraham Lincoln lived.

Abraham Lincoln once lived in New Salem. He worked as a store clerk and postmaster. Later, he became the sixteenth president. He led the country through the Civil War (1861–1865). After the war, African American slaves were freed.

New Salem is a blast from the past. People there cook like Abraham Lincoln would have!

13

Lincoln and a partner owned a grocery store in New Salem. Unfortunately, the store lost money, and they sold it.

President Lincoln issued the Emancipation Proclamation in 1863. It freed some slaves. The Civil War ended slavery for all.

The state capitol took more than 20 years to finish. Twenty-two million bricks were used in the construction.

Springfield and the State Capitol

Illinois is called the Land of Lincoln. Abraham Lincoln spent many years in Illinois. His home, law office, and tomb are in Springfield. He also worked in Springfield's Old State Capitol. Now there's a new state capitol. It houses the state government offices.

Illinois's government has three branches. One branch makes laws. It's called the General Assembly. The governor heads another branch. It carries out the laws. Courts make up the third branch. They see if laws have been broken.

Welcome to Springfield, the capital of Illinois!

Ronald Reagan (1911–2004) was born in Tampico. He was the 40th U.S. president (1981–1989).

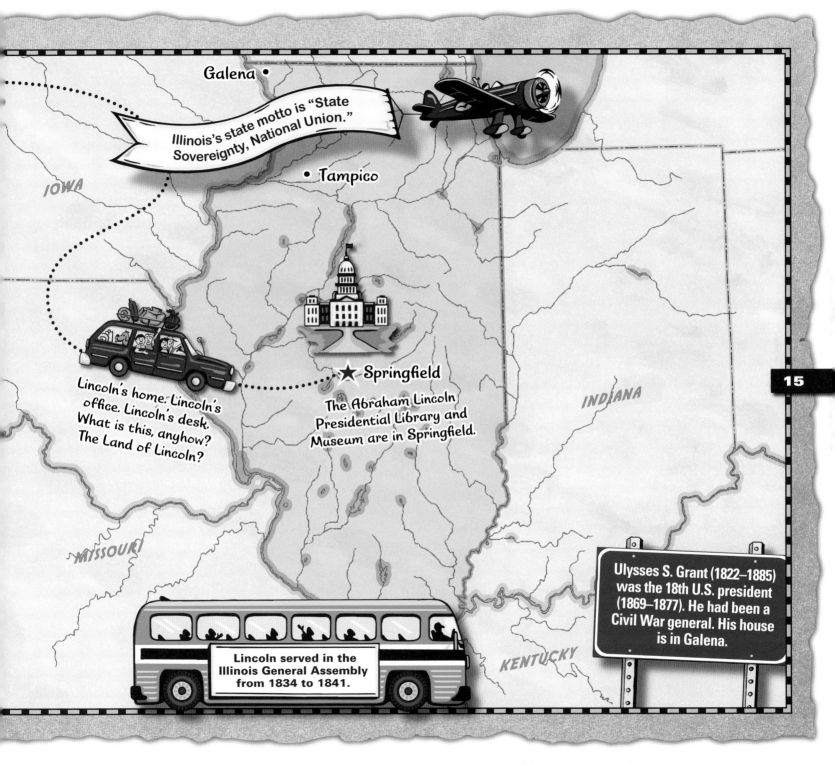

Galena •

Illinois's state motto is "State Sovereignty, National Union."

IOWA

• Tampico

Lincoln's home. Lincoln's office. Lincoln's desk. What is this, anyhow? The Land of Lincoln?

★ Springfield

The Abraham Lincoln Presidential Library and Museum are in Springfield.

INDIANA

MISSOURI

Lincoln served in the Illinois General Assembly from 1834 to 1841.

Ulysses S. Grant (1822–1885) was the 18th U.S. president (1869–1877). He had been a Civil War general. His house is in Galena.

KENTUCKY

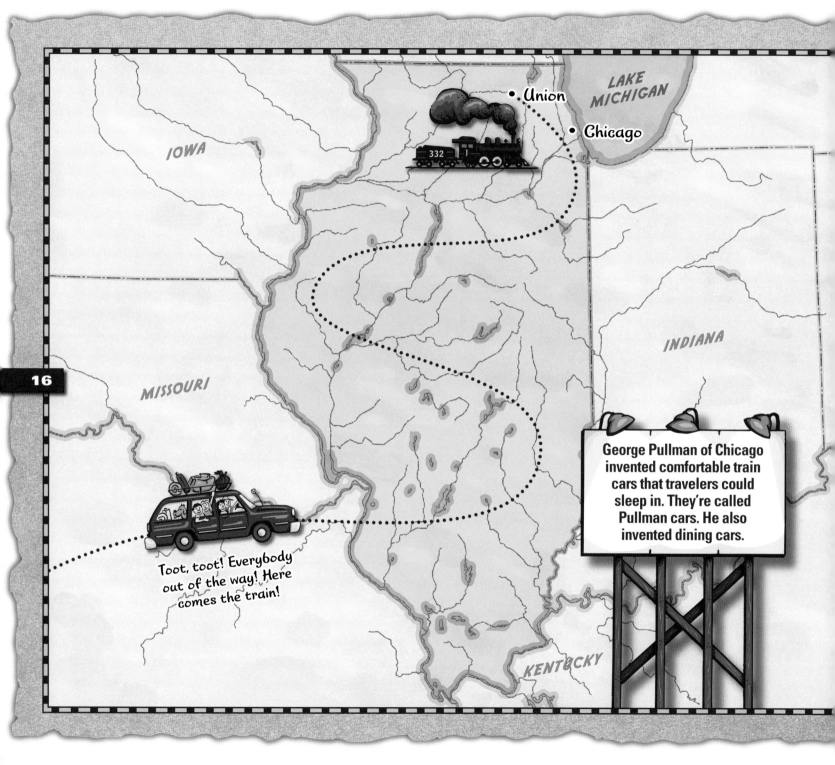

The Illinois Railway Museum

The train's whistling by—and you're on it! You're at the Illinois Railway Museum in Union. It brings back the days when railroads ruled! Visitors get to ride on a real old-time train.

Railroads helped Illinois grow in the late 1800s. Farmers were growing tons of grain. They raised cattle and hogs, too. These products went to Chicago by train. Chicago became the country's center for meat and grain.

Thousands of immigrants came to Illinois. Some worked on farms. Some worked in factories. Others worked in train yards or meat-packing plants.

The Illinois Railway Museum has trains galore! It's the largest railway museum in America.

Let's head over to the Greek booth. I want some calamari!

The Skokie Festival of Cultures

Scoop up some pansit. Grab a couple of falafel. Crunch on some calamari. Then snarf down some masala dosai. You're eating your way around the world. And you never left Skokie! You're at the Skokie Festival of **Cultures.**

Illinois is home to dozens of **ethnic** groups. They include Mexican, African American, and Polish people. Others have roots in Germany, Ireland, Italy, or Asian lands. It's a treat to explore their cultures—and their foods!

Sampling Middle Eastern foods is fun. Hummus and falafel are a yummy combination.

POPULATION OF LARGEST CITIES

Chicago 2,896,016
Rockford 150,115
Aurora 142,990

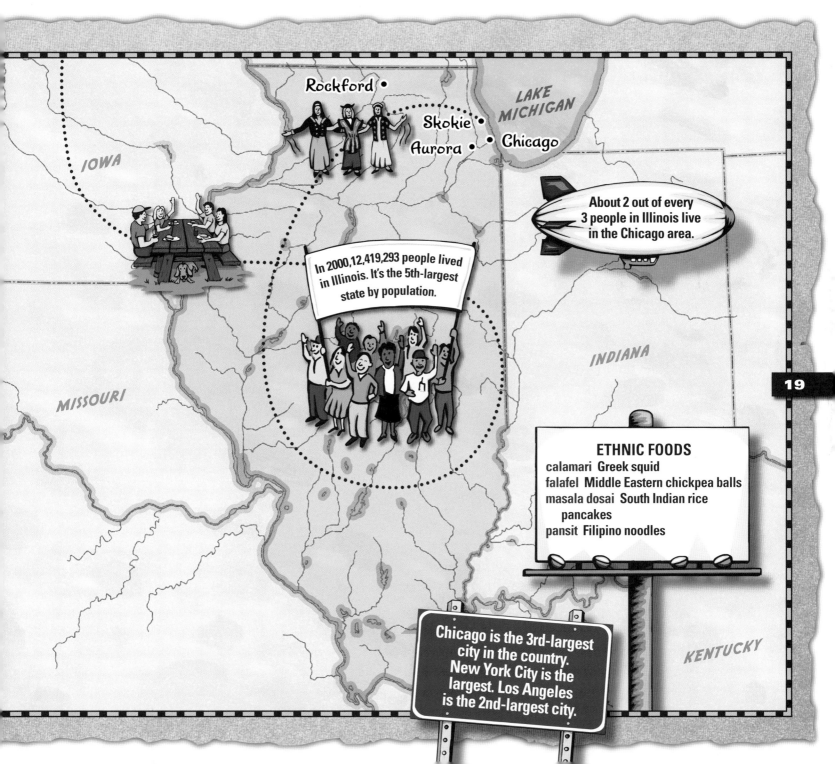

Rockford •

Skokie •

Aurora • • Chicago

LAKE MICHIGAN

IOWA

MISSOURI

INDIANA

KENTUCKY

In 2000, 12,419,293 people lived in Illinois. It's the 5th-largest state by population.

About 2 out of every 3 people in Illinois live in the Chicago area.

ETHNIC FOODS
calamari Greek squid
falafel Middle Eastern chickpea balls
masala dosai South Indian rice pancakes
pansit Filipino noodles

Chicago is the 3rd-largest city in the country. New York City is the largest. Los Angeles is the 2nd-largest city.

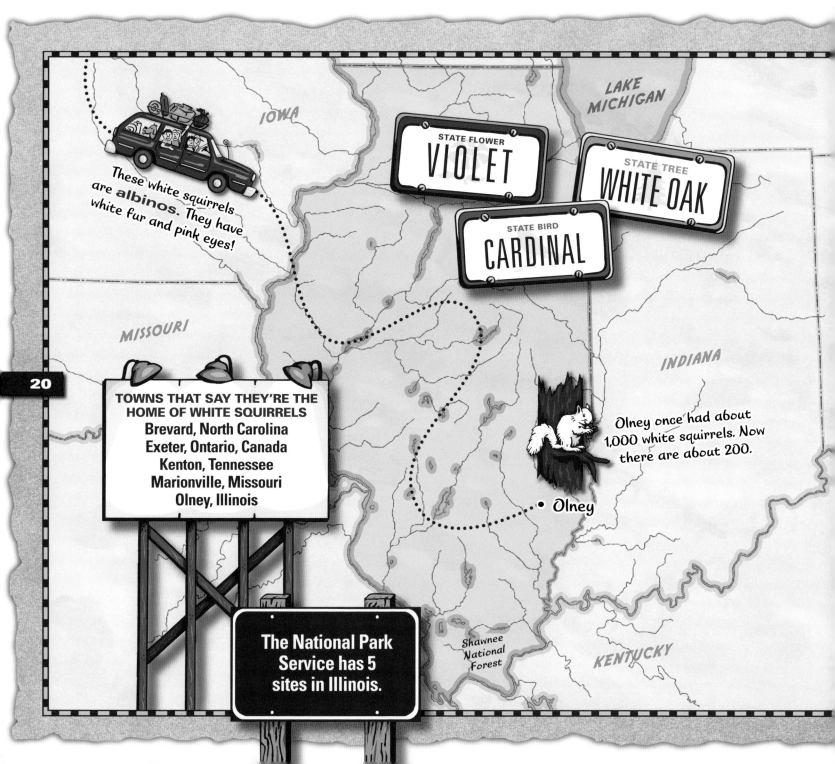

These white squirrels are **albinos**. They have white fur and pink eyes!

STATE FLOWER
VIOLET

STATE TREE
WHITE OAK

STATE BIRD
CARDINAL

TOWNS THAT SAY THEY'RE THE HOME OF WHITE SQUIRRELS
Brevard, North Carolina
Exeter, Ontario, Canada
Kenton, Tennessee
Marionville, Missouri
Olney, Illinois

Olney once had about 1,000 white squirrels. Now there are about 200.

• Olney

The National Park Service has 5 sites in Illinois.

LAKE MICHIGAN

IOWA

MISSOURI

INDIANA

Shawnee National Forest

KENTUCKY

Counting White Squirrels in Olney

There's a white squirrel. Write it down. There are three more. Write those down, too. And don't miss any! It's the yearly white squirrel count in Olney.

People in Olney love their bushy-tailed friends. The squirrels like corn, nuts, and birdseed. Some will eat right out of your hand!

You're more likely to see gray squirrels in Illinois. They scamper around the cities and forests. The thickest forests are in southern Illinois. Deer, raccoons, and foxes live there. Waterbirds love Illinois's lakes, ponds, and rivers. You'll find wild ducks and Canada geese there. But don't try to count them. There are millions!

A white squirrel enjoys a nut. Olney is famous for these furry residents.

Olney police and firefighters wear white-squirrel patches on their uniforms.

Canoe quiz: What's a pudding stick? Answer: A short paddle to use in narrow creeks.

Whoosh. Swish. You're so quiet, the deer don't run away. You're canoeing down the Middle Fork River.

Canoeing is a great way to enjoy Illinois. There are lots of biking and hiking trails, too. Lake Michigan is a fun place in the summer. People fish, swim, and picnic along the shore.

Illinois has some great sports teams. One is the Chicago Bulls basketball team. Its star player was Michael Jordan. He made the Bulls world famous.

Michael Jordan could jump so high that people called him Air Jordan.

22

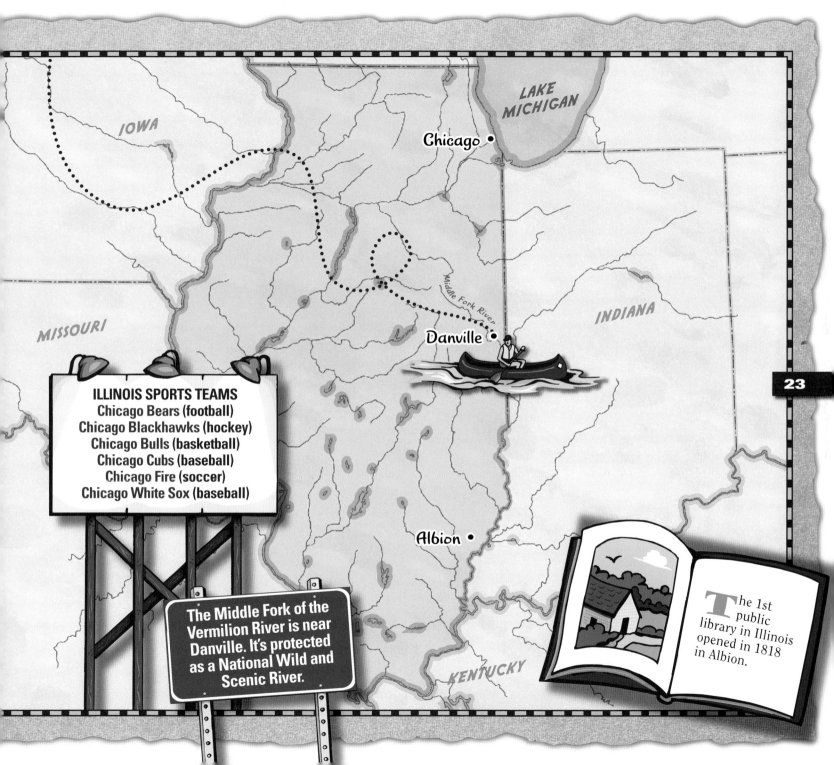

IOWA

LAKE MICHIGAN

Chicago •

MISSOURI

Middle Fork River

INDIANA

Danville •

ILLINOIS SPORTS TEAMS
Chicago Bears (football)
Chicago Blackhawks (hockey)
Chicago Bulls (basketball)
Chicago Cubs (baseball)
Chicago Fire (soccer)
Chicago White Sox (baseball)

Albion •

The Middle Fork of the Vermilion River is near Danville. It's protected as a National Wild and Scenic River.

The 1st public library in Illinois opened in 1818 in Albion.

KENTUCKY

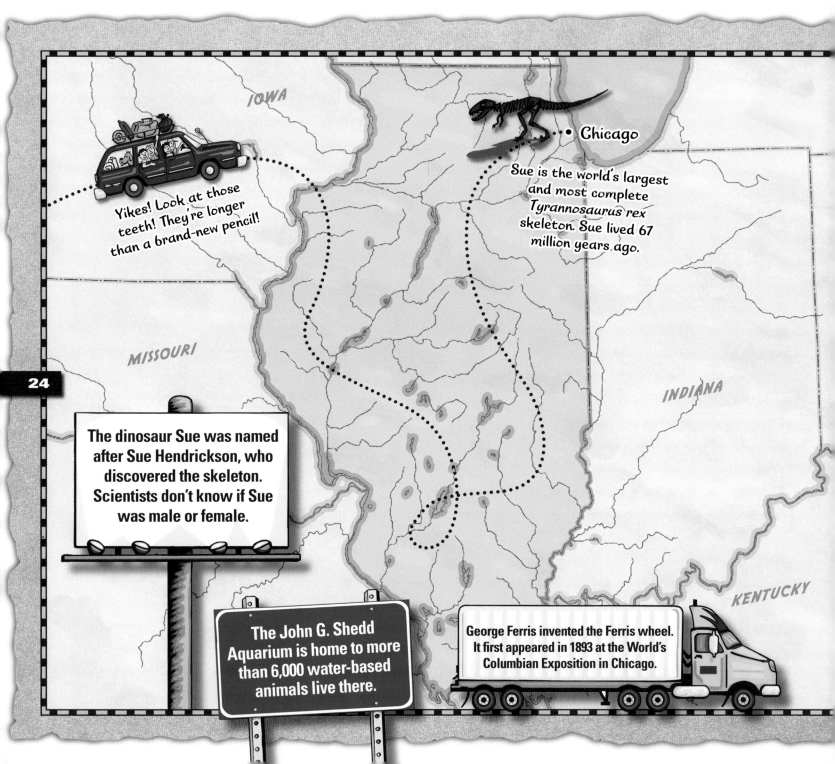

IOWA

Chicago

Yikes! Look at those teeth! They're longer than a brand-new pencil!

Sue is the world's largest and most complete *Tyrannosaurus rex* skeleton. Sue lived 67 million years ago.

MISSOURI

INDIANA

The dinosaur Sue was named after Sue Hendrickson, who discovered the skeleton. Scientists don't know if Sue was male or female.

KENTUCKY

The John G. Shedd Aquarium is home to more than 6,000 water-based animals live there.

George Ferris invented the Ferris wheel. It first appeared in 1893 at the World's Columbian Exposition in Chicago.

Chomp. There goes a **rib cage.** Chomp. There goes a head. Watch out! It's Sue, the *Tyrannosaurus rex.* She could chomp you in one bite! If she were alive, that is. Sue's skeleton is all that's left. It's at Chicago's Field Museum of Natural History.

Sue was discovered in 1990. The scary skeleton was found in South Dakota.

Chicago is full of fun things to do. See a baby whale at Shedd Aquarium. Watch a sky show at Adler Planetarium. Ride the Ferris wheel at Navy Pier. Want to tour a coal mine? Or walk through a human heart? That's easy. Just visit the Museum of Science and Industry.

The Adler Planetarium was the 1st planetarium in the Western Hemisphere.

25

Fermi did his 1942 tests in a lab beneath the University of Chicago soccer field.

Ask-a-Scientist Tour at Fermilab

26

Want to know how matter and energy work? Visit Fermilab to find out.

Enrico Fermi's tests led to the atom bomb. The United States used atom bombs to end World War II (1939–1945).

What are MACHOs and WIMPs? They're objects in outer space! You'll learn all about them on Fermilab's Ask-a-Scientist tour.

Fermilab is the Fermi National Accelerator Laboratory. It's named after Enrico Fermi. He did tests with **atoms** in Chicago. In 1942, he produced **nuclear energy.** Soon, Illinois became an important center for nuclear science.

Argonne National Laboratory is another science center. It's in the town of Argonne. Its scientists study atoms, energy, and many other things!

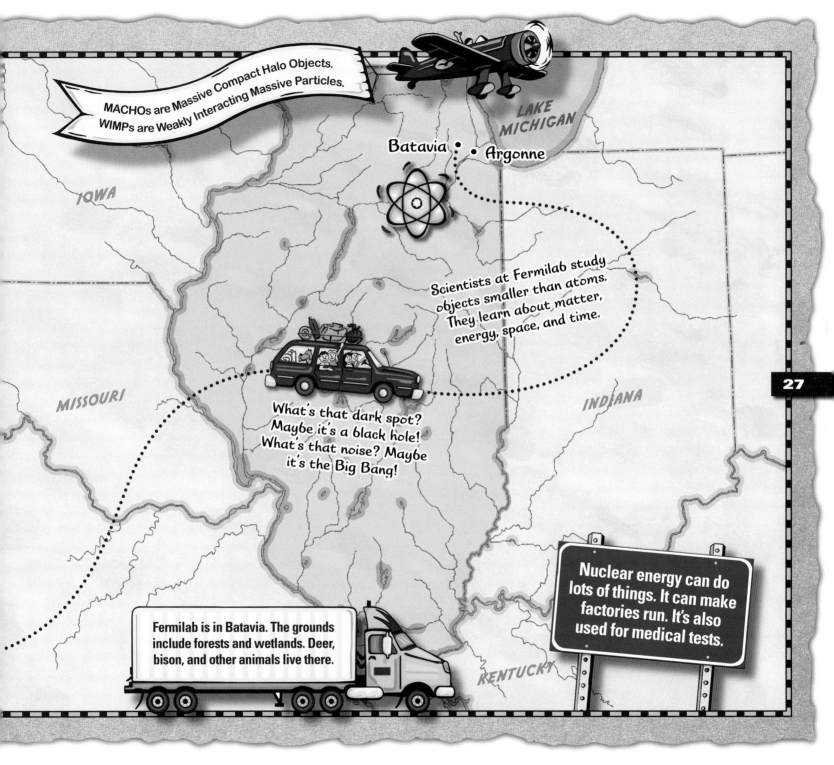

MACHOs are Massive Compact Halo Objects. WIMPs are Weakly Interacting Massive Particles.

Batavia • • Argonne

Scientists at Fermilab study objects smaller than atoms. They learn about matter, energy, space, and time.

What's that dark spot? Maybe it's a black hole! What's that noise? Maybe it's the Big Bang!

IOWA

MISSOURI

LAKE MICHIGAN

INDIANA

KENTUCKY

Fermilab is in Batavia. The grounds include forests and wetlands. Deer, bison, and other animals live there.

Nuclear energy can do lots of things. It can make factories run. It's also used for medical tests.

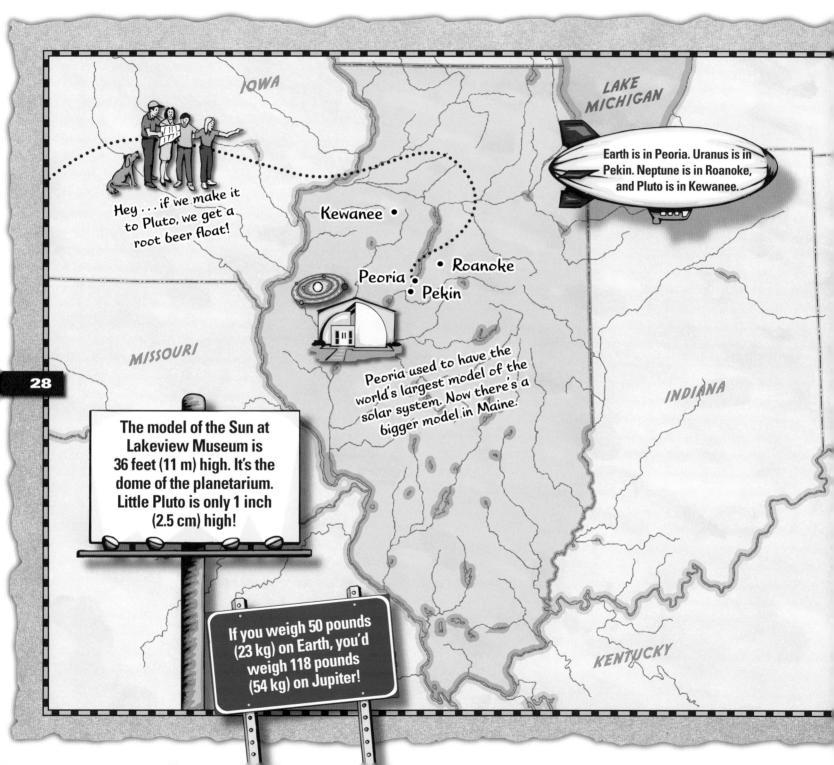

Hey ... if we make it to Pluto, we get a root beer float!

Earth is in Peoria. Uranus is in Pekin. Neptune is in Roanoke, and Pluto is in Kewanee.

Peoria used to have the world's largest model of the solar system. Now there's a bigger model in Maine.

The model of the Sun at Lakeview Museum is 36 feet (11 m) high. It's the dome of the planetarium. Little Pluto is only 1 inch (2.5 cm) high!

If you weigh 50 pounds (23 kg) on Earth, you'd weigh 118 pounds (54 kg) on Jupiter!

Bike Riding Around the Solar System

Hop on your bike at the Sun. Ride to Jupiter and back. Two billion miles? No big deal. How about a trip to Pluto and back? That's 14 billion miles! No problem. You're on the Interplanetary Bike Ride in Peoria!

Lakeview Museum of Arts and Sciences holds this event. The museum built a model of the solar system. That's our Sun and its nine planets. The model had to be exact. So some "planets" are placed miles apart. What about Pluto, the most distant planet? It's at a furniture store in another town!

Lakeview Museum has it all. See paintings and sculptures or learn about science.

In Peoria's solar system model, 1 mile (1.6 km) represents 125 million miles (201 million km).

The Great American Popcorn Company makes more than 80 flavors of popcorn!

The Great American Popcorn Company

Like popcorn? Head to Galena for a taste treat!

Walk down the streets of Galena. Pretty soon you'll smell some yummy flavors. Just follow your nose. Where does it take you? To the Great American Popcorn Company!

Inside, you watch the corn poppers at work. You watch the coaters add special flavors. And you get free samples. Yum! It's still hot!

Illinois is one of the top farming states. It's in a region called the Corn Belt. Corn is the state's leading crop. Some of it is fed to farm animals. Illinois's hogs and cattle like it. So do people like you. Just think of corn dogs, corn muffins, and popcorn!

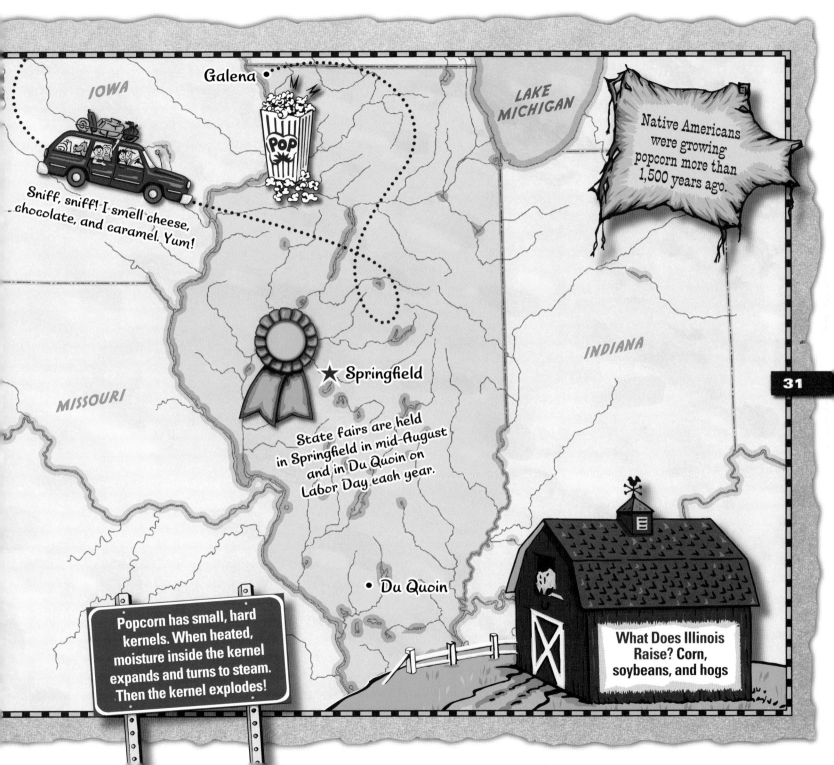

IOWA

Galena

POP

Sniff, sniff! I smell cheese, chocolate, and caramel. Yum!

LAKE MICHIGAN

Native Americans were growing popcorn more than 1,500 years ago.

MISSOURI

★ Springfield

State fairs are held in Springfield in mid-August and in Du Quoin on Labor Day each year.

INDIANA

• Du Quoin

Popcorn has small, hard kernels. When heated, moisture inside the kernel expands and turns to steam. Then the kernel explodes!

What Does Illinois Raise? Corn, soybeans, and hogs

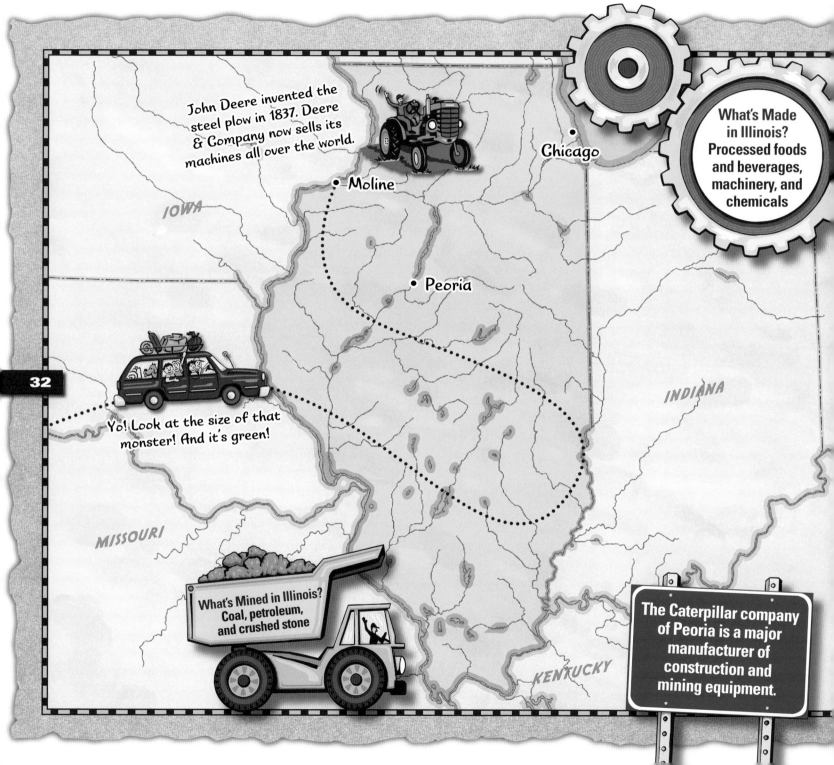

John Deere invented the steel plow in 1837. Deere & Company now sells its machines all over the world.

Chicago

Moline

IOWA

Peoria

What's Made in Illinois? Processed foods and beverages, machinery, and chemicals

INDIANA

Yo! Look at the size of that monster! And it's green!

32

MISSOURI

What's Mined in Illinois? Coal, petroleum, and crushed stone

KENTUCKY

The Caterpillar company of Peoria is a major manufacturer of construction and mining equipment.

The John Deere Pavilion

Visitors can climb right onto some of the farm machinery in Moline.

Are you into monster machines? Like tractors with wheels taller than you? Just visit the John Deere Pavilion in Moline. You'll see lots of farm machines. Some are gigantic, and some are very old. You'll also learn about farm machine history. Collectors can pick up some model tractors there, too.

Many Illinois factories make machines. Farming and construction machines are important products. Around Chicago, lots of factories make foods. They make baked goods, cereal, and other yummy things.

Cyrus McCormick invented a machine for harvesting wheat in 1831. His Chicago factory became the International Harvester Company.

34

The World's Tallest Man

Robert Wadlow was an inspiration to many people.
He is remembered as a kind person.

Stand by Robert Wadlow's statue in Alton. Your head might be just above his knee. This guy is a giant!

He sure is. He's Robert Wadlow. He grew up to be the world's tallest man. Robert was also kind and friendly. People called him the Gentle Giant.

Robert was a regular kid. The only difference was, he was tall! At thirteen, he was the tallest Boy Scout ever. The other kids came up to his chest. He kept growing in high school. The other students came up to his tummy!

Wadlow wore size 37 shoes. He made goodwill tours for the International Shoe Company.

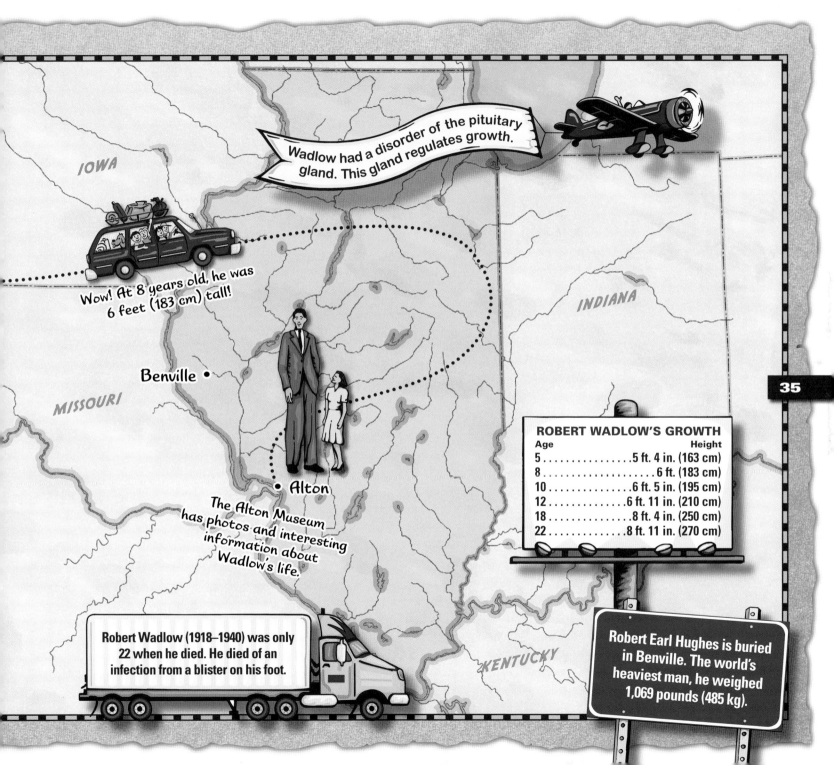

Wadlow had a disorder of the pituitary gland. This gland regulates growth.

Wow! At 8 years old, he was 6 feet (183 cm) tall!

IOWA

INDIANA

MISSOURI

Benville •

• Alton

The Alton Museum has photos and interesting information about Wadlow's life.

KENTUCKY

ROBERT WADLOW'S GROWTH

Age	Height
5	5 ft. 4 in. (163 cm)
8	6 ft. (183 cm)
10	6 ft. 5 in. (195 cm)
12	6 ft. 11 in. (210 cm)
18	8 ft. 4 in. (250 cm)
22	8 ft. 11 in. (270 cm)

Robert Wadlow (1918–1940) was only 22 when he died. He died of an infection from a blister on his foot.

Robert Earl Hughes is buried in Benville. The world's heaviest man, he weighed 1,069 pounds (485 kg).

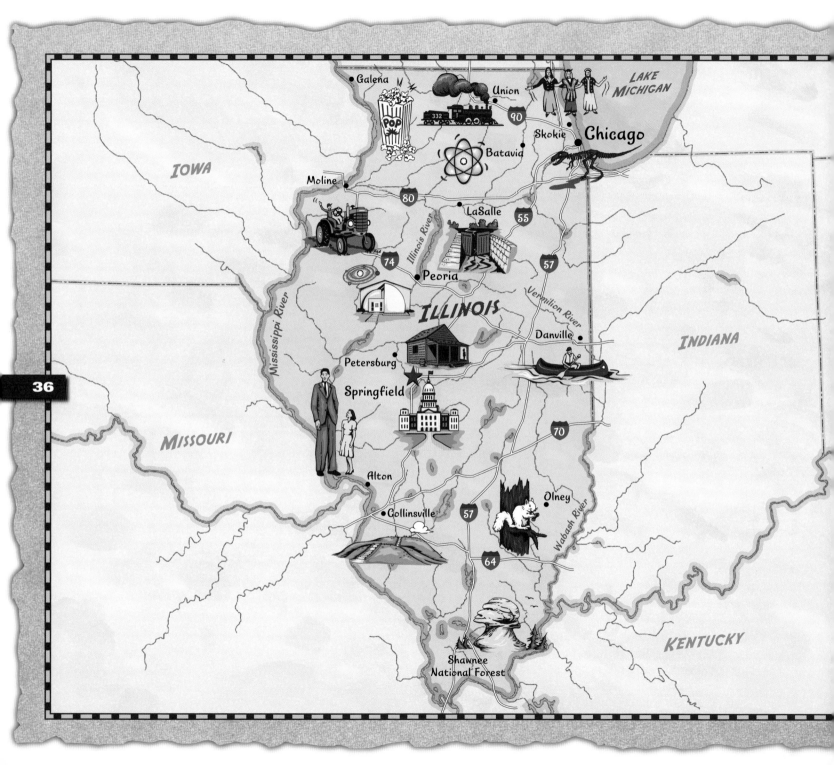

IOWA

Galena

Union

LAKE MICHIGAN

POP

332

90

Skokie

Chicago

Batavia

Moline

80

LaSalle

55

Illinois River

74

57

Peoria

ILLINOIS

Vermilion River

Danville

INDIANA

Petersburg

Springfield

MISSOURI

70

Alton

Olney

Wabash River

Collinsville

57

64

KENTUCKY

Shawnee
National Forest

OUR TRIP

We visited many amazing places on our trip! We also met a lot of interesting people along the way. Look at the map on the left. Use your finger to trace all the places we have been.

Why is Illinois called the Prairie State? See page 6 for the answer.

Where is the world's largest ketchup bottle? Page 9 has the answer.

Which former U.S. president was born in Tampico? See page 14 for the answer.

How many white squirrels live in Olney? Look on page 20 for the answer.

Who is the dinosaur called Sue named after? Page 24 has the answer.

What are MACHOs and WIMPs? Turn to page 27 for the answer.

Who was growing popcorn more than 1,500 years ago? Look on page 31 and find out!

What size shoes did Robert Wadlow wear? Turn to page 34 for the answer.

That was a great trip! We have traveled all over Illinois!

There are a few places we didn't have time for, though. Next time, we plan to visit the Sears Tower in Chicago. This building is the tallest in North America and measures 1,450 feet (442 m). From that high up, you can even see parts of nearby states!

More Places to Visit in Illinois

WORDS TO KNOW

albinos (al-BYE-nohz) animals with white hair, light skin, and pink eyes

atoms (AT-uhmz) tiny bits of matter

burials (BER-ee-uhlz) ceremonies to bury people who have died

cultures (KUHL-churz) customs, beliefs, and ways of life

ethnic (ETH-nik) relating to a person's nation or race

immigrants (IM-uh-gruhnts) people who move from their home country to another country

nuclear energy (NOO-klee-ur EN-ur-jee) a powerful force produced by splitting an atom

prehistoric (pree-hi-STOR-ik) taking place before people began writing down history

rib cage (RIB KAYJ) the set of rib bones around the chest and back

tributary (TRIB-yuh-ter-ee) a river that flows into a bigger river

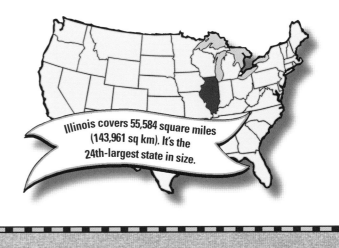

Illinois covers 55,584 square miles (143,961 sq km). It's the 24th-largest state in size.

STATE SYMBOLS

State animal: White-tailed deer

State bird: Cardinal

State dance: Square dance

State insect: Monarch butterfly

State fish: Bluegill

State flower: Violet

State fossil: Tully monster

State mineral: Fluorite

State prairie grass: Big bluestem

State tree: White oak

State flag

State seal

STATE SONG

"Illinois"

Words by C. H. Chamberlain, music by Archibald Johnston

By thy rivers gently flowing, Illinois, Illinois,
O'er thy prairies verdant growing, Illinois, Illinois,
Comes an echo on the breeze.
Rustling through the leafy trees, and its mellow tones are these,
    Illinois, Illinois,
And its mellow tones are these, Illinois.

From a wilderness of prairies, Illinois, Illinois,
Straight thy way and never varies, Illinois, Illinois,
Till upon the inland sea,
Stands thy great commercial tree, turning all the world to thee,
    Illinois, Illinois,
Turning all the world to thee, Illinois.

When you heard your country calling, Illinois, Illinois,
Where the shot and shell were falling, Illinois, Illinois,
When the Southern host withdrew,
Pitting Gray against the Blue, there were none more brave than
    you, Illinois, Illinois,
There were none more brave than you, Illinois.

Not without thy wondrous story, Illinois, Illinois,
Can be writ the nation's glory, Illinois, Illinois,
On the record of thy years,
Abraham Lincoln's name appears, Grant and Logan, and our
    tears, Illinois, Illinois,
Grant and Logan, and our tears, Illinois.

FAMOUS PEOPLE

Addams, Jane (1860-1935), social services leader

Black Hawk (1767-1838), Sauk Indian chief

Brooks, Gwendolyn (1917-2000), poet

Clinton, Hillary (1947-), senator

Davis, Miles (1926-1991), jazz trumpeter and composer

Earp, Wyatt (1848-1929), frontier lawman

Goodman, Benny (1909-1986), composer and bandleader

Grant, Ulysses S. (1822-1885), 18th U.S. president

Hickok, Wild Bill (1837-1876), frontiersman

Jordan, Michael (1963-), basketball player

Lincoln, Abraham (1809-1865), 16th U.S. president

McCully, Emily Arnold (1939-), author and illustrator

Murray, Bill (1950-), movie star

Peck, Richard (1934-), children's author

Reagan, Ronald (1911-2004), 40th U.S. president

Silverstein, Shel (1932-1999), poet and illustrator

Sosa, Sammy (1968-), baseball player

Sturges, Preston (1898-1959), film director and writer

Waters, Muddy (1915-1983), blues musician

Wells-Barnett, Ida B. (1862-1931), journalist, civil rights leader

TO FIND OUT MORE

At the Library
Bielski, Ursula, and Amy Noble (illustrator). *Creepy Chicago: A Ghosthunter's Tales of the City's Scariest Sites.* Chicago: Lake Claremont Press, 2003.

Santella, Andrew. *Illinois Native Peoples.* Chicago: Heinemann Library, 2003.

Somervill, Barbara A. *Illinois.* New York: Children's Press, 2001.

Wargin, Kathy-Jo, and Gijsbert van Frankenhuyzen (illustrator). *L Is for Lincoln: An Illinois Alphabet.* Chelsea, Mich.: Sleeping Bear Press, 2000.

Winter, Jonah, and Jeanette Winter (illustrator). *Once Upon a Time in Chicago: The Story of Benny Goodman.* New York: Hyperion Books for Children, 2000.

On the Web
Visit our home page for lots of links about Illinois:
http://www.childsworld.com/links

Note to Parents, Teachers, and Librarians: We routinely verify our Web links to make sure they are safe, active sites—so encourage your readers to check them out!

Places to Visit or Contact
Chicago Historical Society
1601 N. Clark Street
Chicago, IL 60614
312/642-4600
For more information about the history of Illinois

Illinois Bureau of Tourism
James R. Thompson Center
100 W. Randolph Street
Suite 3-400
Chicago, IL 60601
800/226-6632
For more information about traveling in Illinois

INDEX

Bye, Prairie State.
We had a great time.
We'll come back soon!

DISCARD